PYGMY HIPPOS

ON THE TRAIL

STUDYING
**SECRETIVE
ANIMALS**
IN THE WILD

by Joyce Markovics

CHERRY LAKE PRESS

Published in the United States of America by Cherry Lake Publishing Group
Ann Arbor, Michigan
www.cherrylakepublishing.com

Reading Adviser: Marla Conn, MS Ed., Literacy specialist, Read-Ability, Inc.
Content Adviser: Gabriella Flacke, DVM, MVSc, PhD
Book Designer: Ed Morgan

Photo Credits: © freepik.com, cover and title page; © freepik.com, TOC; © newphotoservice/
Shutterstock, 4–5; © Gabriella Flacke, 5; © freepik.com, 6; © Gabriella Flacke, 7 top; © freepik.
com, 7 bottom; © freepik.com, 8; © Anan Kaewkhammul/Shutterstock, 9; © Keung/Shutterstock,
10 top; © David Moreno Hernandez/Shutterstock, 10 bottom; © freepik.com, 11; © Olga Miltsoba/
Shutterstock, 12; © Gabriella Flacke, 13; © stockfoto/Shutterstock, 14; © andrey oleynik/Shutterstock,
15 bottom left; Retouch man/Shutterstock, 15 bottom right; © belizar/Shutterstock, 16; © jeep2429/
Shutterstock, 17; © fivepointsix/Shutterstock, 18; © Scarabea/Shutterstock, 19; © visa netpakdee/
Shutterstock, 20; © Rose Waddell/Shutterstock, 21; Gabriella Flacke, 22; © Ron Magill, 23; © Yatra/
Shutterstock, 24; © IBREAM/ibream.org in partnership with Prof. Kone and Ouatarra, 25; © freepik.com,
26–27; © spatuletail/Shutterstock, 28; © freepik.com, 29; freepik.com, 31.

Cherry Lake Press is an imprint of Cherry Lake Publishing Group.

Library of Congress Cataloging-in-Publication Data

Names: Markovics, Joyce L., author.
Title: Pygmy hippos / by Joyce L. Markovics.
Description: First edition. | Ann Arbor, Michigan : Cherry Lake Publishing,
   [2021] | Series: On the trail: studying secretive animals in the wild |
   Includes bibliographical references and index. | Audience: Ages 10 |
   Audience: Grades 4-6
Identifiers: LCCN 2020030351 (print) | LCCN 2020030352 (ebook) | ISBN
   9781534180499 (hardcover) | ISBN 9781534182202 (paperback) | ISBN
   9781534183216 (ebook) | ISBN 9781534181502 (pdf)
Subjects: LCSH: Pygmy hippopotamus—Juvenile literature.
Classification: LCC QL737.U57 M375 2021 (print) | LCC QL737.U57 (ebook) |
   DDC 599.63/5—dc23
LC record available at https://lccn.loc.gov/2020030351
LC ebook record available at https://lccn.loc.gov/2020030352

Printed in the United States of America
Corporate Graphics

CONTENTS

HIDDEN HIPPOS

In 2013, wildlife **veterinarian** Gabriella "Gaby" Flacke was hiking through the Taï Forest in West Africa. It was hot and sticky. "Sometimes it felt too hot to breathe," says Gaby. She ducked under branches and dodged tangles of tree roots. Monkeys looked down at her from the **canopy**. Snakes dangled from trees like vines. Spider webs large enough to catch basketballs stretched across her path.

A forest in Ivory Coast

LOOK CLOSER

The Taï Forest is located in a country called Ivory Coast, or Côte d'Ivoire. **Pygmy** hippos also live in Guinea, Sierra Leone, and Liberia—all of which are in West Africa.

Gaby was excited to see animals all around her. "What an incredible place, where the wildlife comes to you," she says. However, the one creature Gaby was searching for was nowhere in sight. Where was the mysterious pygmy hippopotamus hiding?

Veterinarian Gabriella "Gaby" Flacke holds a baby pygmy hippo at a zoo. "I've loved hippos since I was a small child," she says.

THE SEARCH CONTINUES

Gaby headed deeper into the forest, hoping to find the **elusive** pygmy hippo. Holding a tree branch for balance, she crossed a small river. There are waterfalls and rivers throughout the Taï Forest. Pygmy hippos are semiaquatic, living partly on land and partly in the water. This is one of the reasons the forest is prime hippo **habitat**.

Pygmy hippos can hold their breath for up to 5 minutes.

A pygmy hippo trap

Up ahead, Gaby saw a pygmy hippo trap along the bank of the river. The trap, a large boxlike structure made from sticks, was set up by other members of Gaby's team. It's used to safely catch the animals for a brief period in order to study them. However, the trap was empty. Gaby checked a hidden camera set up near the trap. The footage showed porcupines, hogs, and small antelope called duikers. "No signs of pygmy hippos, though," she says. Would Gaby ever see one?

LOOK CLOSER

Pygmy hippos are mammals. Even though they look like large pigs, their closest living relatives are whales and dolphins!

UNIQUE ANIMALS

Gaby was not surprised it was taking so long to spot a pygmy hippo. Few people have ever seen these creatures in the wild. For one thing, the hippos are shy and live alone in **remote** rainforests in West Africa. Also, they're active mainly at night. During the day, the hippos rest in rivers or pools in the forest.

LOOK CLOSER

Hippopotamus comes from Greek words meaning "river horse."

At first glance, pygmy hippos look like smaller versions of common hippopotamuses, also known as river hippos. But they're different in many ways from their larger cousins, says Gaby. Pygmy hippos weigh 10 times less than common hippos. And they spend less time in the water. As a result, their toes are spread out. They are built more for walking than for swimming. Also, their eyes are on the sides, not the tops, of their heads. This helps the smaller hippos **survey** their environment.

A common hippo weighs 3,000 to 9,900 pounds (1,361 to 4,491 kg).

A pygmy hippo weighs 350 to 600 pounds (159 to 272 kilograms).

SPECIAL SKIN

Pygmy hippos have greenish-black skin that blends in with their forest homes. Their shiny skin is up to 2 inches (5 centimeters) thick and has a rubbery feel. It's also covered with tiny bumps. Each bump is connected to a tiny **gland** under the skin that oozes a white, oily fluid. This fluid turns into a foamy lather when it comes into contact with other surfaces. "It leaves soap-like suds floating on the water's surface," says Gaby.

Pygmy hippo skin

Hippo secretions look like soapsuds in the water.

The white fluid, or secretion, protects pygmy hippos' skin. It's like built-in sunscreen made just for hippos. In addition, the white fluid keeps the hippos' skin from drying out in the hot African sun. According to Gaby, the secretions help protect the skin from **infections** and insect bites.

Pygmy hippo ear and lip hair

LOOK **CLOSER**

Pygmy hippos only have hair on the tips of their ears, lips, and tail. It's coarse and feels like bristles on a hairbrush!

TUSKS AND OTHER TEETH

Both pygmy and common hippos have tusks, which are large **canine** teeth. Tusks are mainly used for defense. Hippos often show their teeth by "yawning" at their enemies, such as leopards, or at other hippos. Gaby says that when males are fighting, the yawn can mean: "Don't mess with me, or you'll get to see these up close!" Hippos rarely use their teeth to attack other animals "unless it's a **territorial** battle," says Gaby.

Scientists think pygmy hippos may also use their tusks to carve out places to rest in riverbanks.

The other teeth in pygmy hippos' mouths are for eating. The animals are **herbivores** and eat "a **myriad** of different shoots, leaves, ferns, seeds, and fruits," Gaby says. They look for food at night and in the early morning, when it's cool out. Using their noses, they sniff the forest floor, searching for something tasty. However, Gaby and other scientists still don't know the full range of the pygmy hippo's diet.

Pygmy hippos mostly feed on land.

LOOK **CLOSER**

Each pygmy hippo has a territory. Males are thought to have larger territories than females. They use their tail like a paddle to fling dung and urine on plants and rocks. They do this to mark their home ranges.

PYGMY HIPPO SIGHTING

Finally, after many weeks in the Taï Forest, Gaby got to see a pygmy hippo. "I almost hit the ceiling with excitement when we saw a video, recorded by our camera trap, of a real-life pygmy hippo!" says Gaby. The hippo, a male, was eating a yam that Gaby and her team had placed in the trap as **bait**. Unfortunately, the hippo was hesitant and didn't come all the way into the trap. But he did return to the trap.

A young male pygmy hippo

"The next night, the cameras showed the very same hippo visiting the trap again," says Gaby. The problem was that a hungry porcupine had stolen the yam! When the hippo showed up, he was sniffing around for the missing treat.

Video footage of a pygmy hippo

Yams used as bait for the pygmy hippos

LOOK **CLOSER**

There are many African folktales about pygmy hippos. One story tells of a hippo carrying a diamond in its mouth at night. The diamond is said to have lit its path in the forest.

FAMILY TIME

Wild pygmy hippo babies, or calves, are even harder to study than adults, says Gaby. Male and female hippos only come together to **breed**. Breeding can occur throughout the year. After about 7 months, the female hippo gives birth to the calf on land. A newborn pygmy hippo weighs around 13 pounds (6 kg). That's about as much as a large watermelon!

A newborn pygmy hippo calf

For the first few weeks of the calf's life, the mother hides her tiny baby in the forest. She returns four or five times a day to feed the calf. Scientists think that after a few months, the baby joins its mother in the forest. The calf grows fast. After about 5 months, it weighs around 100 pounds (45 kg)!

A mother and her growing baby

LOOK CLOSER

Mother pygmy hippos help their calves learn how to be in water without drowning. Hippos don't actually swim. They walk along the bottom of a river or pond and push themselves up to the water's surface to breathe air.

AT RISK

Sadly, the places where pygmy hippo families live are under threat. "Pygmy hippos are only found in a very small area of unique tropical habitat in West Africa," says Gaby. Many of the forests where the animals make their homes are being logged or burned. This is being done to make way for farming and mining. In just 50 years, 70 percent of the forest in Ivory Coast has been destroyed. That's one of the highest **deforestation** rates in the world.

A farmer burns logs from a destroyed rainforest.

A woman chopping meat from wild animals, known as bushmeat, at a local market

Hunting is another threat to hippo survival. People enter the forest and often **illegally** kill wild animals for food. Some people in Africa don't have enough food to eat. Some experts think that pygmy hippos may be targeted for their tasty flesh. Although the exact number is unknown, Gaby says there are fewer than 2,500 pygmy hippos living in the wild.

LOOK **CLOSER**

Pygmy hippos are an endangered species, which means they're at risk of dying out.

ZOO LIFE

Nearly 10 percent of all pygmy hippos left in the world live in zoos. Because the animals are so endangered, zoos are an important way to help save the **species**. Luckily, pygmy hippos appear to thrive in zoos, and many male and female hippos have successfully bred in zoos.

This pygmy hippo rests in a pool at a zoo.

Zoo Basel in Switzerland keeps track of all the breeding pygmy hippo pairs and births in zoos around the world. In recent years, the number of calves born under this kind of managed care has doubled. Since 1928, over 70 pygmy hippo calves have been born at Zoo Basel alone. Because the animals are so hard to study in the wild, zoos help scientists like Gaby learn more about these elusive hippos.

A zoo worker observes a mother and new calf at ZooTampa, Florida.

LOOK **CLOSER**

The first pygmy hippo was brought to Europe from West Africa in 1873 but died within a few hours of arrival. In 1912, several pygmy hippos were brought to a zoo in Germany and then to the Bronx Zoo in New York. These animals flourished.

GABY'S WORK

Today, Gaby works as a zoo vet studying and helping pygmy hippos. She's passionate about uncovering "ways to **optimize** the health, welfare, and breeding" of pygmy hippos. For one project, Gaby collected dung samples from hippos around the world. Then she measured levels of certain chemicals in the dung. This helped her and other experts learn about the animals' stress levels, health, and **reproduction**.

Gaby collecting dung

As part of her job, Gaby also **operates** on sick animals. In 2019, she and a team of doctors operated on the mouth of a young pygmy hippo named Aubergine. The **palate** of the 150-pound (68 kg) calf was **deformed**. This caused food to come out of Aubergine's nose and led to infections. "We want him to live as good of a life as he can," says Gaby.

Gaby and baby Aubergine, which is another word for eggplant

LOOK **CLOSER**

Aubergine might need additional operations in the future to fix his deformed palate.

SAVING HIPPOS

While zoos are important **conservation** tools, much more needs to be done, says Gaby. The places where pygmy hippos live must be protected. "With less suitable habitat come fewer and fewer pygmy hippos," she says. Creating large areas of protected land—and replanting forests—in West Africa can help the long-term survival of the species. But Gaby says there is only one way conservation will ever work. That's if the people who share the forests with the hippos have food, jobs, and their basic needs met.

Education is another way to help save the precious pygmies. Children are the future leaders of the world. Inspiring them to care about pygmy hippos and the forests where the creatures live is key. In Ivory Coast, kids celebrate Hippo Day to raise awareness about the hippos and their conservation.

Children celebrating Hippo Day in Ivory Coast with a model of a pygmy hippo

LOOK **CLOSER**

Hippo Day celebrations include a parade. Kids also write poems and songs about hippos and their habitat.

THE FUTURE

Every day, Gaby is reminded that there is still much to learn about pygmy hippos. A lot of what scientists would like to know about the animals has yet to be discovered. But she's determined to learn everything there is to know about them. That will take time, and time is running out.

Without further efforts, pygmy hippos could disappear from the wild altogether. They live in the "last **remnants** of West Africa's declining rainforests," says Gaby. "These forest **enigmas** are silently clinging to life." Even though pygmy hippos are rarely seen, they shouldn't be forgotten.

LOOK CLOSER

The oldest known pygmy hippo lived to be 50 years old. His name was Hannibal, and he lived at the Stuttgart Zoo in Germany.

FAST FACTS

PYGMY HIPPOS

Scientific Name
Choeropsis liberiensis

Physical Description
Shiny greenish-black skin with short, coarse hair on lips, ears, and tail

Size
Up to 6 feet (2 m) long and 30 to 39 inches (76 to 99 cm) tall

Weight
350 to 600 pounds (159 to 272 kg)

Main Diet
Shoots, leaves, ferns, seeds, and fruits

Habitat
Forests in Liberia, Ivory Coast, Guinea, and Sierra Leone

Life Span
35 to 50 years in zoos; it's not known how long pygmy hippos live in the wild

DID YOU KNOW?

- A pygmy hippo named Billy was given to U.S. President Calvin Coolidge in 1927. Almost all pygmy hippos living in American zoos today are related to Billy.

- Pygmy hippo calves can drink milk from their mothers on land and underwater!

- According to some West African folklore, pygmy hippos were once human beings.

- Pygmy hippos pinch their nostrils and ears tightly shut to keep out water when they dive underwater.

GLOSSARY

bait (BAYT) food used to attract an animal to a trap

breed (BREED) to come together to have young

canine (KAY-nine) the sharp, pointy teeth found on the sides of the upper or lower jaw

canopy (KAN-uh-pee) the top layer of leaves and branches covering a forest

conservation (kahn-sur-VAY-shuhn) the protection of wildlife and natural resources

deforestation (dee-for-ih-STAY-shun) the process of cutting down forests

deformed (dih-FORMD) misshapen or disfigured

elusive (ih-LOO-siv) very hard to catch or find

enigmas (uh-NIG-muhz) puzzling things

flourished (FLUR-ishd) developed in a healthy or successful way

gland (GLAND) a body part that produces chemicals

habitat (HAB-ih-tat) the natural home of an animal or plant

herbivores (HUR-buh-vorz) plant-eating animals

illegally (ih-LEE-guhl-ee) forbidden by law

infections (in-FEK-shuhnz) illnesses caused by germs entering the body

myriad (MIR-ee-uhd) a great number of things

operates (AH-puh-rates) cuts open a body to repair a damaged or diseased part

optimize (AHP-tuh-mize) to make as effective or useful as possible

palate (PAL-it) the roof of the mouth

pygmy (PIG-mee) something very small for its kind

remnants (REM-nuhnts) remaining small parts

remote (rih-MOHT) difficult to reach

reproduction (ree-pruh-DUHK-shuhn) the act of producing babies

species (SPEE-sheez) a group of similar animals that can reproduce with each other

survey (sur-VAY) to carefully look around

territorial (ter-uh-TOR-ee-uhl) involving the area where an animal lives and finds its food

urine (YOOR-uhn) liquid waste produced by animals

veterinarian (vet-ur-uh-NER-ee-uhn) a doctor who cares for animals

READ MORE

Arnold, Caroline. *Hippo*. Great Neck, NY: Seymour Science, 2013.

Rake, Jody Sullivan. *Hippos in the Wild*. Mankato, MN: Capstone Press, 2010.

Walker, Sally M. *Hippos*. Minneapolis: Lerner Publications, 2008.

LEARN MORE ONLINE

IBREAM: Pygmy Hippo Awareness Activities
   https://ibream.org/updates/pygmy-hippo-awareness-activities-2018

San Diego Zoo: Pygmy Hippopotamus
   https://animals.sandiegozoo.org/animals/pygmy-hippopotamus

YouTube—Zoological Society of London: Adorable Pygmy Hippo Born
   https://www.youtube.com/watch?v=96xC5JIkIpQ

ZooTampa: Pygmy Hippo
   https://zootampa.org/animals/pygmy-hippo

INDEX

ABOUT THE AUTHOR

Joyce Markovics has authored more than 150 books for young readers. She's wild about rare and unusual animals and is passionate about preservation. Joyce lives in an old house along the Hudson River in Ossining, New York. She would like to thank Dr. Gaby Flacke for her generous contribution to this book and for her commitment to caring for pygmy hippos.